# Ram

David Farr is a writer and director. His plays *The Danny Crowe Show*, *Elton John's Glasses*, *Night of the Soul*, *The UN Inspector* and a collection of adaptations have all been published by Faber. He was Artistic Director of London's Gate Theatre from 1995 to 1998, and Joint Artistic Director of Bristol Old Vic from 2002 to 2005. He has directed *Coriolanus* and *Julius Caesar* for the RSC and *The UN Inspector* for the National Theatre. In June 2005 he became Artistic Director of the Lyric Theatre, Hammersmith, where his productions have included new versions of *The Odyssey* and Kafka's *Metamorphosis*.

# DAVID FARR

# Ramayana

*a dramatic retelling of the Indian epic*

*faber and faber*

First published in 2007
by Faber and Faber Limited
3 Queen Square, London WC1N 3AU

Typeset by Country Setting, Kingsdown, Kent CT14 8ES
Printed in England by Bookmarque, Croydon, Surrey

A CIP record for this book
is available from the British Library

ISBN 978-0-571-23775-3

2 4 6 8 10 9 7 5 3 1

This book is dedicated to my parents
with love

# Introduction

I first read the *Ramayana* in 1995 on a train from Chennai
to Mumbai. It was a short and wonderfully alive prose
version by the venerable Indian statesman and intellectual
Chakravarti Rajagopalachari. I read it in one sitting –
only interrupted by a ten-year-old boy falling on my head
from the luggage rack above. Since that time I have read
many other versions, poetic and prose. As a regular
director of Shakespeare, I have been constantly struck by
the Shakespearean quality of the story – the exile into the
forest, the mixture of high tragedy and low comedy, the
deep-seated humanism, the themes of romantic love,
grief, loss, spiritual self-discovery and reconciliation.
I have wanted for many years to explore this remarkable
story on the stage.

I finally wrote this dramatic retelling of the *Ramayana*
after a journey to Varanasi in 2006. In doing so, I felt
how strongly the story's exploration of the conflict
between materialism and religion speaks to our time.

For their help and advice I wish to thank Shashank from
the Ganges View Hotel, Varanasi, Pinku Pandry, Ajay
Chaucharia at the Kanak Bhavan Temple, Ayodhya, the
cast and creative team of the opening production, the
Lyric staff, Simon Reade, Angie Bual's mother, and most
of all my fellow traveller through India, Folco Terzani.

David Farr, January 2007

**Ramayana** was first presented at the Lyric Hammersmith, London, on 9 February 2007. A Lyric Hammersmith, Bristol Old Vic and West Yorkshire Playhouse production. The cast was as follows:

**Ram**  Paul Sharma
**Sita**  Vanessa Ackerman
**Ravana/Kaikeyi**  Éva Magyar
**Dasarath**  Nicholas Khan
**Lakshman**  Kolade Agboke
**Hanuman**  Richard Simons
**Sugriva/Shurpanakha**  Stephen Ventura
**Musician**  Marc Layton-Bennett

All other parts were played by the company

*Written and directed by*  David Farr
*Music by*  Shri
*Designed by*  Ti Green
*Movement direction by*  Amit Lahav
*Puppetry by*  Blind Summit
*Lighting by*  Jakie Shemesh
*Sound by*  Nick Manning
*Produced by*  Kate McGrath of Fuel

## A Note on Names

In Northern India the hero of *Ramayana* is
called Ram. In Southern India he is called Rama.
Similarly Dasarath/Dasaratha.

To an English ear the 'a' ending sounds better,
but I have used both versions,
depending on rhythm and metre.

# Characters

**Dasarath,** King of Ayodhya
**Ram,** his eldest son
**Sita,** Ram's wife
**Lakshman,** Ram's brother
**Kaikeyi,** one of Dasaratha's wives
**Two Townsmen** of Ayodhya
**Bharat,** Ram's brother
**Ascetic**
**Shurpanakha,** sister of Ravana
**Ravana,** King of Lanka
**Maricha,** uncle of Ravana
**Jataiyu** the vulture
**Hanuman,** a monkey
**Sugriva,** a monkey, brother of Vali
**Dalit,** a monkey
**Vali,** King of the Monkeys
**Vali's Monkey Wife**
**Monkey of the North**
**Monkey of the East**
**Monkey of the West**
**Sampatu** the vulture
**The Ocean**
**Indrajit,** a trickster

Soldiers, Citizens, Women of Lanka,
Monkeys, Warriors

# RAMAYANA

# Act One

## SCENE ONE

*Two townsmen of Ayodhya.*

**Townsman 1**
Quiet everyone! Listen!

**Townsman 2**
Miraculous news!

**Townsman 1**
King Dasaratha.

**Townsman 2**
Wise man.

**Townsman 1**
Has called a secret council.

**Townsman 2**
He summoned all his eldest Brahmins to him.

**Townsman 1**
They gathered from all corners of the kingdom.
From the mountains and the forests and the plains.
From all Ayodhya came like geese in summer
The Brahmins to his palace.

**Townsman 2**
They sat like children do before a story.

**Dasaratha**
My body rusts. It is time for me to pass.
My eldest son Rama is steadfast as earth.
He is the blessing that Ayodhya needs.
I wish him to become king of Ayodhya.

**Townsman 2**

When the Brahmins heard they burst into waves of
joy . . .

**Townsman 1**

Like peacocks spotting long-awaited rain . . .

**Townsman 2**

They cried –

**Townsman 1**

Let it be now! Rama will safeguard holy Ayodhya.
He pursues dharma. He hunts truth. He is calm.
He is a warrior unsurpassed.

**Townsman 2**

The king frowned.

**Dasaratha**

Why this sudden rush of enthusiasm? Am I not a good
king?

**Townsman 1**

Majesty, you have protected us without a thought for
your own happiness. Old age happens. Give away
your duties now and rest. We love to see Rama. He
gazes on doubt – it disappears. He speaks – he is
believed.

**Townsman 2**

The king smiled.

**Dasaratha**

Then let it be tomorrow. Time presses us to action.
If I wait longer, my mind may become jealous.
Brahmins! Prepare for the coronation!
And bring me my son! He must be first to know.
Only then will I tell the people!

**Townsman 1**

But we were too smart. Someone was listening at the
golden windows. Someone was lurking in the marble

halls. Word spread like fire. The news has leaked! The whole city knows!

**Townsman 2**

And now look! The ancient rooftops are bursting with colour. The streets are sprinkled with flowers and water. The taverns are jam-packed! The shapely courtesans throw open their doors at a special price! The officers buff up their silver shields. The wives prepare their silken gloves. The sick leap from their beds, the lame smash their crutches and dance, misers give away gold, and the kitchens of rich men offer free food to all! The young women of Ayodhya shoot arrows of love from their eyes – they're pining for the night of celebration after our new king is crowned!

**Townsman 1**

Now we wait for Ram himself! His brother Lakshman is fetching him and his wife Sita!

**Townsman 2**

Radiant Sita! Moon-bright Sita!

**Townsman 1**

We will fetch them from their marriage bed . . .

**Townsman 2**

. . . which they are always loath to leave . . .

**Townsman 1**

. . . raise them on an elephant, and our cheers will carry them to his father's palace. Our loving eyes will crown him –

**Townsman 2**

Ram – new king!

**Townsman 1**

Saviour, of Ayodhya!

## SCENE TWO

*Ram and Sita in their private room. Entering to them, Lakshman.*

**Lakshman**
Ram. Brother! Where are you?

**Rama**
                                    Not here.

**Lakshman**
Brother, you must come.

**Rama**
Lakshman this is the private hour.
When a man and a wife share time . . . together . . .

**Lakshman**
                                    But brother –
Have you not heard?

**Sita**
                    Lakshman – it's not like you
To cause embarrassment to a married woman.
You see we are unprepared for your visit.

**Rama**
Leave us. At dinner we can discuss your concerns.

**Lakshman**
But brother . . .

**Rama**
                    At dinner!

**Lakshman**
                            Rama, our father sent me.

*Pause.*

**Rama**

Our father? Why didn't you say so?

**Lakshman**

Come down and I will tell.

**Rama**

                Is he unwell?

**Lakshman**

In body and mind. For days he had bad dreams.
Stars plummeting in a twilight of terror.
Ayodhya burning. Death rushed through the streets,
Plucking people like flies.

**Rama**

Why didn't he tell me?

**Lakshman**

He knew what the dreams meant.

**Sita**

That Ayodhya is doomed unless change is made.

**Lakshman**

Your wife thinks fast. Now he has made the change.

**Rama**

He is abdicating.

**Lakshman**

                Passing the throne to you.

**Rama**

A warrior cannot accept this gift.

**Lakshman**

This is no gift. It is necessity.
Ayodhya is weak and getting weaker.
The holiest city. Now so full of holes,
It's hollow. The Kingdoms of the South threaten us.
Lanka grows in power, makes wealth its weapon,

boasts deep resources, grows, expands. Our ways –
the old rule of the mind – is under threat.

**Rama**

And now my father hopes I will protect it.
Where he has failed, how am I to succeed?

**Lakshman**

The people adore you. Him they merely venerate.

**Rama**

The growth of Lanka and the Southern Kingdoms
Cannot be stopped by servile adoration.
They've money, military might. They offer
Freedoms and pleasures that would tempt any man.
What do I have to offer?

**Lakshman**

Goodness. Justice.

**Rama**

You can't eat justice.

**Sita**

You were expecting this.

**Rama**

I looked into my father's eyes and saw
Ayodhya's light fading.

**Lakshman**

We can revive it.

**Rama**

Not possible. We are in the second age.
All is decaying.

**Lakshman**

Do not believe it.

**Rama**

Can I stand up against it? Against Ravana,

The Southern Kings and their endless hunger?
We are in the era of the grasping fist.

**Sita**

                                        Rama.
Look out the window.

**Rama**

                      The old city.

**Sita**

Long home to great sages, men of spirit.
The echoes of the mantras. The river flowing.
The gods themselves feel at home here. Is this to be lost?

**Rama**

There are flowers on the rooftops.

**Lakshman**

                             They blossom for you.

**Rama**

The air is sweet with sandalwood.

**Sita**

                                It breathes for you.

**Rama**

Wooden torches tall as trees line the roads.

**Lakshman**

They burn for you, my brother.

**Rama**

Has the city ever looked so beautiful? My home.
It is like gazing on an old story – when Ayodhya
Was the cradle of all life. When it was life!

**Lakshman**

Shall be again.

**Sita**

When I married you, I married Ayodhya.

**Rama**

Sita dress me in gold. Take me to my father.
Carry me high through the streets. Let the roar of
Ayodhya echo to the southern lands – Rama is King!

### SCENE THREE

*Kaikeyi's room in Dasaratha's palace. Kaikeyi, Dasaratha
entering to her.*

**Dasaratha**

Why this darkness? My whole palace is ablaze
With light and colour. Banners from every wall.
Flowers cascade down stairs. Music and song
Fill every room, chanting the name of Ram!
I walked here through a festival of light.
My wives' chambers a riot of red and pink,
Silver and green. Every window a golden lantern!
Except one. One dark window. One black room.
Kaikeyi, my dearest, sweetest wife of all,
Creature of infinite pleasure – explain this darkness!

*Pause.*

Kaikeyi! Dasaratha speaks! Where are you?
Where are your lotus blossoms? Where your sticks
Of incense? Where your singing? Kaikeyi!

*Kaikeyi reveals herself, stripped, covered in soot, lying
on the ground.*

What is this? Wife – explain this degradation!
This is a day of rapture!

*Pause.*

                    Why this silence?

*Pause.*

Speak!

**Kaikeyi**

        Bharata.

**Dasaratha**

             Bharata is our son.
He is away in Rajgira.

**Kaikeyi**

                          You sent him there.

**Dasaratha**

He is safe with your family. What is this about?

**Kaikeyi**

You got him out of the way. So Ram shall be king.

**Dasaratha**

What are you suggesting? Bharat and Ram are
brothers. Their love is stronger than death.

**Kaikeyi**

                                  Kausalya's son.
Preferred to mine.

**Dasaratha**

Not preferred – older. Rama is greatly loved.
It is right he should be king. Get up from the ground.

**Kaikeyi**

You removed my son.

**Dasaratha**

                    He went of his own free will.
Get up.

**Kaikeyi**

        Not until . . .

**Dasaratha**

                  Make yourself decent!

*Pause.*

**Kaikeyi**

Do you desire me?

**Dasaratha**

Always. You above all.

*He tries to touch her. She stops him.*

You are unwell. I will call my physicians.
They will attend upon you.

**Kaikeyi**

It is you who will require their assistance.

**Dasaratha**

You speak in riddles.

**Kaikeyi**

How is your memory?

**Dasaratha**

I age. Why ask?

**Kaikeyi**

Do you remember this?
On the battlefield. You were young. Brave – fearless.
You fought with Indra against the Asuras.
A thunderbolt knocked you unconscious to the ground.
Death was imminent. I carried you, I alone,
Ran to the field of war, I saved you, I protected you,
Nursed you back to life. I did this. Did I not?
Such was my love. And what did you promise me?

**Dasaratha**

Wife, do not ask . . .

**Kaikeyi**

To reward me for my love . . .

**Dasaratha**

Kaikeyi do not . . .

**Kaikeyi**

You promised me two wishes . . .

**Dasaratha**

Do not ask this.

**Kaikeyi**

For whenever I might need them.
Two wishes that cannot be refused.

*Beat.*

**Dasaratha**

My queen. You whom I love above all others,
Desire above all others . . .

**Kaikeyi**

King of Ayodhya,
I request the first wish.

**Dasaratha**

Do not request it!

**Kaikeyi**

My first wish is that you pass on the crown,
Not to your son Rama, but to our son, Bharata.

**Dasaratha**

The world sings Rama's virtues. Ayodhya needs him.
Do not do this.

**Kaikeyi**

Do you grant me my wish?

**Dasaratha**

Wife . . . Kaikeyi . . .

**Kaikeyi**

Do you grant me my wish?

**Dasaratha**

You know that if you wish it I must grant it.

**Kaikeyi**
I wish it.

**Dasaratha**
Then it is granted. Oh my city.

**Kaikeyi**
King of Ayodhya, I request the second wish.

*Pause.*

**Dasaratha**
What now?

**Kaikeyi**
I wish that Ram be banished from the kingdom
Into the forests for fourteen years.

**Dasaratha**
In wishing this you murder Dasarath.

**Kaikeyi**
Do you grant me my wish?

**Dasaratha**
What jealousy
Has inflamed you?

**Kaikeyi**
Do you grant me my wish?

**Dasaratha**
I beg of you, turn back. Turn back from this terror.

*Pause.*

**Kaikeyi**
This behaviour dishonours you. Lying there
Like a child. You promised me a second wish.
Do you grant it? Or do I have to slit my throat?

**Dasaratha**
You know . . . . I have to grant it . . . if you wish it.

**Kaikeyi**
I wish it.

**Dasaratha**
Then it is granted.

*Pause.*

And I will never see my son again.

**Kaikeyi**
Now I will light my chamber. Call the palace.

**Dasaratha**
You call them. Dasaratha's mouth stops here.

*Enter Rama, Sita and Lakshman, with Townsmen
following, spying on the action.*

**Townsman 2**
Ram approaches the palace!

**Townsman 1**
On a golden elephant he comes like the sun. He seeks
his father.

**Townsman 2**
Grab any spot you can to hear what passes between
them!

**Townsman 1**
Oh joyous day! May Rama rule Ayodhya for ever!

**Rama**
Father?

*Kaikeyi lights up the room.*

**Rama**
Where is the king?

**Kaikeyi**
There. In the corner.

15

**Rama**

You asked to see me, sir.
                          Thousands of people
Are singing in the streets. What do they know?
Tell me your desire – I am ready to fulfil it.

*Pause.*

Is my father angry? Have I done something to hurt him?
Tell me so that I can repair the damage.
I cannot bear you suffering like this.

**Kaikeyi**

King Dasaratha has something he must tell you.

*Pause.*

**Rama**

What is it? Father?

*Dasarath does not speak.*

**Kaikeyi**

                          When you were still a child,
I saved your father's life. He granted me
Two wishes for whenever I should need them.
Today I have that need.

**Rama**

                          What is your wish?

**Kaikeyi**

That you give up the throne to my son Bharata.
You leave here and as a beggar for fourteen years
Live in the forests. With no earthly riches.

**Rama**

And did he grant your wish?

**Kaikeyi**

                          He did.

**Lakshman**

Did you, Father?

*Dasarath nods.*

**Rama**

If this is my father's wish, then I accept.
Prepare me for my exile.

**Lakshman**

Rama! The city!

**Rama**

The city is nothing but Dasaratha's desire.

**Lakshman**

But without you Ayodhya will crumble.
Seize the kingdom now! Kill this serpent
Before news of her treachery spreads!

**Sita**

I can do
Better than that. I'll kill her for you.

**Kaikeyi**

You try!

**Lakshman**

I'll kill you, witch, with my own bare hands.
And then I'll slay Bharata and all his men
And anyone who stands against us!

**Rama**

No.
I want to go to the forest. Why weep, Father?
I rejoice in obeying your desires.

**Sita**

Then I come too.

**Rama**

The forest is not for you.

**Sita**

This is a forest without you.

**Rama**

                    Sita. You must
Remain a queen in waiting.

**Sita**

                    So I shall.
I shall walk ahead of you, crushing the thorns
With the soles of my feet. What greater preparation?
What could have made you so unlike yourself
That you wished to leave me here? I am your wife
And I will be with you in palace or in forest,
Heaven or Hell. I am only Sita with you.

**Kaikeyi**

He shall take no earthly riches. It is my wish.
And that includes his queen.

**Sita**

                    It shall be so.
Take off my earthly trappings.

*Sita removes her clothes of state and gives them
to Kaikeyi.*

**Sita**

There – now I am no queen.

**Kaikeyi**

Your skin is pale as silver.

**Sita**

Darken it with soil.

*Kaikeyi soils Sita's skin.*

**Kaikeyi**

Your hair is smooth as spun gold.

**Sita**

Matt it with bark.

*Kaikeyi soils Sita's hair.*

**Rama**

Sita. My queen.

**Sita**

Don't grieve. I shine inside.

**Rama**

Lead us to the gates.

**Lakshman**

I'm coming too.

**Rama**

Lakshman.

Ayodhya needs you.

**Lakshman**

Ayodhya's no home for me now.
Our brother Bharata can have it all.
Let it sleepwalk into our enemies' hands
And Lanka with the fanning of its plumes
Nod you into despair! Besides, you'll need
Someone to build shelters and gather fires.
You were never any good at that.

*Lakshman prepares himself.*

**Rama**

I wish to see my mother.

**Kaikeyi**

There is no time.

*He kisses his father's feet.*

**Rama**

In this as in all things I honour you.

**Dasaratha**

Stop.

**Rama**

Your words are deeds.

**Dasaratha**

Stop.

**Rama**

People of Ayodhya! All the love you bear me,
Bear it for Bharata. Summon him back
From Rajgira. He is a noble man.
Though young in body, old in mind. Let him rule.
Lead us to the city gates.

**Townsman 1**

No, Rama! Stay with us! Or let us come with you!

**Townsman 2**

Let the beasts of the forest invade Ayodhya and let us
follow Ram!

**Townsman 1**

We'll make a new kingdom in the jungle!

**Rama**

Stop this pathetic bawling! My banishment
Is my father's wish and it shall be obeyed.
Lead us to the edge of Chitrakuta forest.
And leave us there.

*The Townsmen lead Rama, Sita and Lakshman to
the city gates and into the forest until the lights of
Ayodhya have disappeared.*

# Act Two

*The forest of Chitrakut. A hut. Lakshman, Rama, Sita.*
*Sita plays with the birds.*

**Lakshman**

Rama, wake up! Sita has gone! Where is she?
What if a wolf has stolen her while we slept?

**Rama**

Calm, brother. Look. Up in the tree.

*Sita is playing with the birds.*

She's made friends with the chakravaka birds
That cry in the night when they have lost their love.
They bring fresh flowers for her royal neck
And deck her in a natural jewelry.
The sharp-eyed forest knows it holds a queen.
Wild animals bow to her. The trees stand sentry,
The moon smiles down and dissipates the darkness,
The sky turns slowly, opens bright its eyes,
And falls in love as I first fell in love
And have been falling ever since. With Sita.

*A noise in the forest.*

Who's this?

**Lakshman**

Lights in the trees. Prepare to fight.

**Rama**

Bharata.

**Lakshman**

Come to kill you. Take your weapon.

Fearful of your return, Bharata moves.
He brings an army fit to conquer Lanka
He wants you out of the picture.

**Rama**

                                    Lakshman, calm.

**Lakshman**
I'll soak the soil in blood. Not one shall live.
The elephants will drag away their corpses.
The birds of prey I'll personally invite
To feed upon his eyes, that dares to try
To fix Ayodhya's crown upon his head.

**Rama**
This is your brother you are talking about!
He loves us.

**Lakshman**
                    I see no love.

**Rama**
                              When has he harmed us?
When has he thought us wrong?

**Lakshman**
                              Then why the horses?
Why fifty thousand men? Why shields? Why swords?
They approach. We have to make our move.

**Rama**
Do nothing.

**Lakshman**
                    Can you not hear their feet!

**Rama**
Do nothing.

**Lakshman**
                    They shake the ground of Chitrakut!
We have to fight. Sita – inside the hut!

**Rama**
    Sita! Do nothing!

**Lakshman**
                  Inside the hut!

**Rama**
                                Don't move!

**Lakshman**
    Sita!

**Sita**
            Lakshman, I seem not to be moving.

**Lakshman**
    You're crazier than him. They are upon us!

*Enter Bharata, in royal apparel, with Attendants. He
falls to his knees at Rama's feet.*

**Bharata**
    I here give up my throne. My crown. My army.
    I bring it all here with me.

**Rama**
                        Brother, welcome.
    Why are you here? Against our father's wishes.

**Bharata**
    Our father has no wishes. He is dead.

**Rama**
    You should be ruling the city. Ensuring law.
    Putting the truth back to the top . . .
    What did you say? Bharata? Did you say dead?
    Dasaratha dead?

**Bharata**
              Of grief. His heart cracked open.
    We heard it echo in the palace halls.

*Rama falls.*

**Rama**

Please. Leave me here. Closer to where he is.
Fetch me some water, Sita. Dead of grief?
And I could do the same. I was not there
To oversee last rites. I was not there.

**Bharata**

He died with just one name upon his lips.

**Rama**

Fourteen years will no longer be enough.
How can I ever return?

**Bharata**

You must. And now.

**Rama**

No! Never! Water, Sita! Now I pour it.
Never return.

**Bharata**

Rama, the city needs you.
When we were young we spoke of all the threats
Ayodhya faced. Of disbelief, of blindness.
People are poor. They need the light of truth
Or else the shining glint of gold will lure them.
My mother's jealousy is an infection,
It catches on the breeze, then all are smitten.
Lanka has gold to burn. People will turn to it
As to a sun if we with greater light
Do not give guidance.

**Rama**

I have no light to give.

**Bharata**

Then all is lost.

**Rama**

No, Bharata. Obey your father's wish.

That remains truth. For fourteen years you must
With all your guts reign king. Suffer the pain
Of seeing the city crumble, keep on suffering,
Knowing the rightness of the path you choose.
I will remain here in this wilderness.
Here nature aids man as he reaches out
To God. So maybe she will aid me too.
Winter will settle with no sign of man.
The solitude of forest floors will be
My way to penance and to better life.
Maybe, when fourteen years have passed, this grief
Will have passed also. Who knows? Fate dictates.
Then I'll return to rule with you.

**Bharata**

                            I'm not strong enough.
To do this all alone.

**Rama**

                You must be strong.
You are the city walls.

**Bharata**
Give me your sandals.

**Rama**

               Well, a strange request.

*Rama gives him the sandals.*

**Bharata**
I will return and place these on the throne.
And at your feet I will govern Ayodhya
As king and slave at once. In fourteen years
You come and fill these shoes. Then will return
Greatness to the oldest city of them all.
I go back!

*Exeunt Bharat and train.*

**Rama**

See, Lakshman. There was nothing much to fear.
Oh Father. Oh my Sita. Oh Dasaratha!

*Enter a group of Ascetics.*

**Lakshman**

Who comes now?

**Sitaa**

An ascetic. Welcome him.

**Ascetic**

You have intruded on our austerities.
Your care of life destroys our privacy.

**Rama**

Hermit, we are sorry.

**Ascetic**

This was a place of holy purity,
Free of the world and its humanity.
We came here to the man-free river, stood
For forty months without moving an inch
Waist-deep in water, raising up our arms
To praise the sun in lonely salutation.
Now all is shattered. Now the protective veil
That kept the demons and the dangers out
Is torn. No longer is this place secure.
Demons will come, Lanka's forces too,
To rape the forest, rip the heart from the earth.
The spell is broken. Nothing we can do
But seek another haven. You must too.

*He exits, as do the other Ascetics.*

**Lakshman**

We must move further into the forest.

**Sita**

Winter is coming, We must a find a home.

26

**Rama**

So long as I am with you, I am home.

*They move further into the forest.*


SCENE TWO

*Deeper in the forest. The female demon Shurpanakha.*

**Shurpanakha**

I've never been this deep in the Dandaka forest before. Those wretched holy men built an invisible wall to keep us out. Killjoys! Then last night the wall cracked open – and now – freedom to explore! Look at all this wilderness. Such potential for development! I never understood the attraction of the natural look. If you have a canvas, why not paint the picture?

I'll go and tell my brother. Lanka is desperate for new terrain to exploit. No resource scarcity here! Oh, he'll love me. Presents for Shurpanakha! I must rush back to Lanka.

*She turns to run back. But sees Rama sitting sadly. Sita and Lakshman sleep.*

Although on the other hand . . . let's not be hasty.

Religious extremists aren't usually my type, but this one . . . is in a completely different spiritual league. Look at those eyes. Not so much a worshipper as a god. And such sweet sadness. Oh yes, I'll pray at that shrine.

You, sir. Devout man. May I offer consolation?

**Rama**

Can you bring fathers back from the grave?

**Shurpanakha**

In grief?
A waste of an emotion. Don't look back.
Move forward. With me. Life won't seem so bad.

**Rama**

Who are you?

**Shurpanakha**

My name's Shurpanakha. Sister of Ravana.
But mistress of myself. I am free to roam
Free in this forest. Free in mind and body.
And free to tell you. I am in love with you.

**Rama**

You don't know who I am.

**Shurpanakha**

Details, details.
All right then. Who are you?

**Rama**

My name is Rama.
This is my brother sleeping. And here my wife.

**Shurpanakha**

An ugly creature. Visibly deformed.
I hope that sleep is deep. With that face.
It would be better if she never woke again.
Now I, on the other hand . . . when I go to bed
'Tis not to doze. You get my drift? Look here.
Look at this stunning nose. Look at these breasts.
Feel free. Indulge. And leave this winsome fairy.
I'll make a man of you.

**Rama**

I'm sure you could.
But I alas am faithful.

**Shurpanakha**

                       Tiresome boy.
Why be constrained by these civilities?
You know you want to. Why resist desire?

**Rama**

All I was thinking was, a woman like you
Would not enjoy to share a man with another,
And not a pallid shadow such as her.
My brother is not spoken for. Shall I wake him?

**Shurpanakha**

Hmmn. Not such thrilling beauty. But built like a tree.
All right. I'm not proud. Wake him up.

**Rama**

Lakshman! Wake up and see your heart's desire.

**Shurpanakha**

Over here, young man.

*He sees her.*

**Lakshman**

What the . . .?

**Rama**

I know. She's quite a vision. And all for you.

**Lakshman**

Get her away from me!

**Shurpanakha**

What is he saying?

**Rama**

Bowled over by desire. He fears what most he wants.
Be soft with him. He's inexperienced.
Lakshman, be tactful to this gracious woman.
Admit your love for her.

**Lakshman**

> Gentle lady.
>
> Lovely as a lotus, sweeter than wine.
> Forgive my seeming horror. I can explain it.
> You are too beautiful for such as me.
> Ram is the king and you are fit for him.

**Shurpanakha**

> Quite right, of course. But what about the wife?

**Lakshman**

> He'll leave her in a trice. Ask and she's gone.

**Shurpanakha**

> Is it true? Would you abandon her for me?

**Rama**

> I long to, but my honour disallows me.
> Lakshman has no impediment. Go with him.

**Lakshman**

> Why court the stars when you can have the sun?

**Rama**

> Why snub a star today for a sun tomorrow?

**Shurpanakha**

> You drive me mad with this absurd debate.
> But I have a solution to our problem.
> I will devour the little sleeping virgin.
> And then the sun'll be free to burn me up.

*She tries to devour Sita. Sita wakes.*

**Rama**

> Lakshman, stop her!

**Lakshman**

> Away from her, you devil!

*Lakshman cuts off her nose.*

**Shurpanakha**

What have you done? My nose! My beautiful nose!
You will regret this, you, your brother and your whore!

*She leaves.*

**Sita**

What kind of game was this? Playing with desire?

**Lakshman**

We did not know she was so dangerous.

**Sita**

I heard a story of a pacifist
And a trick that cruel Indra played upon him.
Indra asked the sage to look after his sword.
The pacifist refused, but Indra begged
To guard it in his hand so none could use it.
Indra left. The pacifist got used to the sword.
Without knowing the reason for his actions
He started trying out the warlike postures.
The thrust, the parry and the slice. Until
At last the thought of violence entered him
And soon the thought translated into deed.
And so he went to Hell.

**Rama**

                    Forgive me, Sita.

**Sita**

What else?
But what will come of this frivolity?

## SCENE THREE

*Ravana's palace on Lanka. Shurpanakha.*

**Shurpanakha**
Betrayal! Revenge! Ravana!

**Ravana**
                                        What is it?

**Shurpanakha**
Look what these vermin did to me? My nose!

**Ravana**
It's not there.

**Shurpanakha**
                        That's because it's here! Cut off!

**Ravana**
My surgeons can replace it. They do everything.

**Shurpanakha**
That's not the point. The point is, I've been slighted.
Humiliated. Laughed at. Scorned. What damage
To my pride. And to yours. My noble brother.
I insist upon revenge. Tear them apart.
Rip limb from limb. And as for the wretched girl,
Take her and show her every violence.
Leave her a piece of meat upon the ground.

**Ravana**
All right, calm down. I'll send some men. Where are
    they?

**Shurpanakha**
In Chitrakuta forest. There are two of them.
Two miserable brothers. Rama and Lakshman.
Weak, ugly cowards both. No match for you.

**Ravana**
Rama? Did you say Rama?

**Shurpanakha**
And you must go yourself. I want blood revenge.

**Ravana**
Did you say Rama?

**Shurpanakha**
Yes, so what?

**Ravana**
Rama of Ayodhya. He is blessed by gods.
No one can touch him.

**Shurpanakha**
Are you saying the mighty power of Lanka
And all its forces are no match for that squeak?

**Ravana**
We are no match for gods. Not yet at least.
I know my limits.

**Shurpanakha**
But I want revenge!

**Ravana**
The time will come. When Ayodhya loses faith,
When the people lose the lustre of belief,
Then we attack. We raze the impregnable city.
We rip all lingering prayers out of their throats
And smash their stupid idols on the stone.
But now is too soon. Do not ask me again.

**Shurpanakha**
It's such a shame. I was only thinking of you.
The girl, you see. She's quite a delicacy.

**Ravana**
Her name?

**Shurpanakha**
Sita. Of the earth. But of unearthly beauty.
Ah well. 'Tis not to be. Never mind.

**Ravana**

Describe her.

**Shurpanakha**
Her hair falls with the silence of a river,
Her eyes are pools so wide that for a man
To dive inside is to fall into dreams.
She conjures in her stunning arching brow.
Her breasts are high, her hips are made for spreading,
None in your harem can light a candle to her.
She is a cure to all the restlessness,
The itching rage that lingers in your mind.
The never-sated curiosity.
All this her moonlit skin can ease away.

**Ravana**
And she is with them both in Chitrakuta?

**Shurpanakha**
Her soft head sleeping on the bare rough ground.
No need to fight him. She's the victory.
But if you're not interested . . .

**Ravana**

Call my uncle to me.

**Shurpanakha**
Of course, my lord. Dear Uncle Maricha!
Your king has something to discuss. Man's stuff.

*Exit Shurpanakha.*

**Maricha**
Great king.

**Ravana**

I need your help. There is a woman

Somewhere deep in the forests of Chitrakut.
I want her to be my wife.

**Maricha**

Another wife?

**Ravana**

My only wife. The rest are decoration.
I want to take her not by force but guile.
I need to use your powers.

**Maricha**

I can transform into anything you require.

**Ravana**

A deer. A many-coloured deer. Of beauty
Irresistible. That when she sees it
Her reasonable mind is intoxicated
And she must have it.

**Maricha**

What is the woman's name?

**Ravana**

Sita, wife of Rama.

**Maricha**

Lord, do you know what you do?

**Ravana**

I want that woman.

**Maricha**

You steal Rama's wife,
You start a blaze that you cannot control.

**Ravana**

I have to have that woman.

**Maricha**

You know how it will end? With mansions burning.

**Ravana**

How long have we waited to defy Ayodhya?

**Maricha**

And we must wait still longer.

**Ravana**

No, not so.
If I can persuade this vision to be my wife.
Not by brute force, but by my charms and by
The glimmer of our freedoms, then as goats after sheep
The rest will follow.

**Maricha**

What if you do not succeed. If she resists?

**Ravana**

Then Rama's wrath will pour upon our heads
And we will fight like dogs.

**Maricha**

The risk is too great.

**Ravana**

I want that woman. Do what I command.


SCENE FOUR

*The forest of Chitrakuta. A many-coloured deer.*

**Sita**

Look, Rama. Have you ever seen such beauty?
Look at its pearly belly. Its emerald face.
Oh, I must have it. Get it for me, Rama.

**Lakshman**

What if it's a trick?

**Sita**

Don't be so silly, Lakshman.

This deer has enraptured me. Get it for me,
My noble hero! He can be our pet.

**Rama**
How can I refuse those eyes?

**Sita**

You have no need.

**Lakshman**
But Rama, I am sure this is some demon
Sent to deceive us.

**Sita**

Rama, please explain.
Why has your brother become such a coward?

**Rama**
Stay here, Lakshman. Guard Sita with your life.
Do not on any account leave her.

**Lakshman**

I swear it.

**Rama**
I will return with your delight.
And we will ride together on its back!

*Exit. Rama chases the deer. He kills it and Maricha
cries in Rama's voice:*

**Maricha**
Lakshman! Help me!

**Sita**

That was my lover's voice.
Lakshman go to him.

**Lakshman**

You heard his orders.
I must not leave your side.

**Maricha**

Lakshman! Help me!

**Sita**

Do you not hear him call? He is your brother!
My husband! Wounded! Dying, maybe dead!
Get after him!

**Lakshman**

I will not leave your side.

**Sita**

You gutless wretch! Disgrace to your family!
How can you sit and hear that and do nothing!
Oh, I know why. You want him to be in trouble.
You want his death. Ah, now I understand.

**Lakshman**

What are you saying?

**Sita**

You've always been jealous.
Of him and me. You only followed us
Into this forest so you could get rid of him
And have the wide-eyed Sita to yourself.

**Lakshman**

Mistress, where do these thoughts come from?
It is the deer that has enchanted you!

**Sita**

I've seen the way you look at me. At my body.
That's what's behind this seeming loyalty.
Lust for this flesh. But this flesh has loved a god,
Honey-skinned Rama. And you think after him
I'd entertain the thought of little Lakshman!

**Lakshman**

Now that's enough! You're just like every woman.
Capricious! Fickle, never satisfied!

**Sita**

You're just like every man except my Rama.

**Lakshman**

You shut your mouth or I will shut it for you!

**Sita**

Ah, now the truth! If you don't want to have us
You want to kill us. Wasn't it ever thus!

**Lakshman**

Another word and I will kill you now!

**Sita**

Another second's wait, I'll kill myself!
I'll throw myself into the holy river!
I'll drink snake poison! Throw myself on rocks!
I'll hack myself to bits before you touch me!

**Lakshman**

No, wait!

*He draws a circle round Sita and blesses it.*

The man who breaks into this circle dies.
Do not set foot outside this sacred bound.

**Sita**

Just go! Time flies and Rama needs your help!

*Exit Lakshman. Enter Ravana, disguised as an Ascetic.*

**Ravana**

I walk the forest path, oh lord, to praise you.
And every creature on the path I love
As every creature bears a piece of you.

**Sita**

Who are you? Please be welcome.

**Ravana**

I thank you, lady.

**Sita**

And when my husband returns from the hunt,
Which I pray god he does and does unharmed,
We'll feast you as is right for a holy sage.

**Ravana**

Sweet lady, has your husband left you here
Alone inside this dark and dangerous forest?
This is the place of demons. Why risk you here?
You should be in a palace wrapped in silks
And all your walks should be in perfumed gardens.
Your slender waist and tapering thighs could tempt
A lesser man to lose his sacred mind
And commit horror.

**Sita**

                    Fear not, wise ascetic.
I am safe here in this circle.

**Ravana**

                    So it is blessed?

**Sita**

With a spell mortal to any man who would break it.

**Ravana**

Then all my fears are answered. What relief.
Lady – I am thirsty. May I take some water?

**Sita**

Wise sir, I may not leave this circle to serve it you.

**Ravana**

And my austerity precludes me fetching it.
No matter. I will wait.

**Sita**

                    You seem to faint, sir.

**Ravana**

It's nothing.

**Sita**

        No, you fall.

**Ravana**

                        A dizziness.

It will pass.

*Pause.*

**Sita**

Please check the forest. See you any harm?

**Ravana**

None but the singing chakravaka birds.

**Sita**

Then I will fetch you water for your thirst.
I will not have you fainting.

*She leaves the circle.*

**Ravana**

You are the only water that I need.

**Sita**

What are you doing? What do you want from me?

**Ravana**

To come with me to Lanka, peerless beauty.
My words stall in my throat, ashamed to match
Your incandescence with imperfect sounds.
Your eyes are tinged with roses and your hair
Falls like a summer rain upon your cheeks.
Your body stands a temple in this forest
And I the lucky seeker chance upon it
As one upon a deep and ancient secret
That opens up its naked majesty
Only to those who dare to enter in.

**Sita**

Get off me! Rama! Lakshman! Where are you?

**Ravana**
Chasing a deer that fits your wildest dreams.
I made that deer, and I can make you more,
A park of rainbow does to fawn on you
And I will turn myself into a doe
And be one of them!

**Sita**
Get away from me!

**Ravana**
Ah ha, you struggle! Then I must use force.

**Sita**
Rama! Lakshman! Ah, birds of the forest, help!
Come to your Sita's aid!

*A cacophony of birds. Enter Jataiyu, vulture, king of the birds.*

**Ravana**
What deadly trash are you?

**Jataiyu**
I am Jataiyu, vulture, king of the birds.
You hold our Princess Sita against her will.
And I will not let you take her.

**Ravana**
Won't you now?
Oh, you have made a moving sacrifice
For this princess. You've sacrificed your life.

*He leaps forward and with his weapon attacks Jataiyu.*

*Elsewhere in the forest, Rama and Lakshman meet.*

**Lakshman**
You live!

**Rama**
That was no deer. It was a trick

Designed to lure me away from you and Sita.
Why have you left her?

**Lakshman**

She heard your desperate cry and was distraught.
She forced me out with wild unlikely words
But before I left I drew a ring around her.
That none may enter in.

**Rama**

Where did you draw it? Show me! Fast!

**Lakshman**

Just here where the chakravaka birds . . .
Why has their singing stopped?

*They see the empty circle.*

**Rama**

Where is she? Where is Sita? WHERE IS SHE?!

**Lakshman**

Gone. She was there. She must have left the circle.

**Rama**

We have to find her!

**Lakshman**

How could she have gone?

**Rama**

Trees! Earth! Birds! Tell me, where is Sita?
Answer your king! What have you done with her?
Give her back to me! I command you – give her back
Or I will rip your eyes out of your skulls!

**Jataiyu**

We did not take her.

**Rama**

Who are you?

**Jataiyu**

Jataiyu.
King of the thousand birds of Chitrakut.
I tried to stop him. But he was too strong.

**Rama**

Who? Who was too strong?

**Jataiyu**

I don't know his name.
He took her and he flew away with her.

**Rama**

Where to? Where to?

**Jataiyu**

Above the trees. She screaming like one mad.
He grasps her sacred body to his own.
They fly beyond the leaves . . . I don't see where.

**Rama**

You must have seen! You must have seen!

**Jataiyu**

Oh princess.

*Jataiyu dies.*

**Rama**

You must have seen. You must have seen!

**Lakshman**

He's dead.

# Act Three

*Another part of the forest. Hanuman the Monkey is looking for honey in the ground. He hears the call of a woman above him.*

**Sita**

Rama! Rama, where are you?

*Sita's necklace of flowers floats down and lands on Hanuman's neck. Hanuman admires the necklace.*

**Hanuman**

Thank you, Shiva, Vishnu, Brahma! You shower gifts on the lowest, meekest monkey. Thank you, gods! Thank you, gods!

*He prostrates himself enthusiastically. Two other Monkeys, Sugriva and Dalit, enter and see him.*

**Sugriva**

What on earth are you doing?

**Hanuman**

Thanking the gods for a miracle.

**Sugriva**

Why, what have they ever done for us?

**Hanuman**

They have blessed me with a thing of beauty.

**Sugriva**

Not your face, then.

**Hanuman**

Thank you, gods! Thank you, gods!

**Sugriva**
Dalit, rouse him from his ecstasy.

*Dalit kicks Hanuman, who wakes.*

**Hanuman**
What was that for?

**Sugriva**
Just a spiritual awakening.

**Dalit**
What's that around your neck?

**Hanuman**
Get off. This is for me alone! I am the special chosen
monkey!

**Dalit**
That's a girl's necklace.

**Hanuman**
You're just jealous because they didn't select you.
It floated to me on the breeze and I heard my name
called on the wind. Hanuman! Hanuman! Lowest of
the lowest caste! I choose you for my messenger! Oh
joy! Oh happiness!

*He leaps in happiness and falls over his tail.*

**Sugriva**
Meanwhile, who's got anything to eat?

**Dalit**
Not me.

**Sugriva**
Hanuman?

**Hanuman**
I was digging for honey when the miracle occurred.

**Sugriva**
Did you find any?

*Hanuman shakes his head.*

**Sugriva**
Three months without food! Everywhere poison plants
and dead roots. Oh, to return home to Kishkindha,
where the honeycombs grow!

**Dalit**
Munching on cocoa leaves.

**Sugriva**
To be home with a lovely monkey wife to cook for us!
Banana stew on a bed of fresh leaves with a flagon of
honey wine!

Oh to be home!
Oh to be home!
In Kishkindha!
Oh to be home!
Oh to be home!
In Kishkindha!

Are those flowers edible?

**Hanuman**
Get off my sacred chain!

*They fight viciously, but give up.*

**Sugriva**
Oh, leave him. How I hate this wilderness.

*A bustle in the undergrowth.*

What was that?

**Dalit**
Two figures in rough clothes.

47

**Sugriva**

My brother's spies. Coming to kill us! Hide!

*Hanuman is still admiring his necklace.*

Hanuman! Hide!

**Hanuman**

Why should I hide? When I have sacred protection?

*They try to pull him into the undergrowth.*

**Sugriva**

Get in, you primate!

**Hanuman**

Shiva will protect me! Let me go!

*Sugriva abandons Hanuman. Enter Rama, Lakshman.*

**Rama**

Why does this forest torment me? Every flower looks like Sita's eyes. Every vine is her hair. Every branch her slender neck, around which the chakravaka birds hung that heavenly . . . that heavenly . . .

*He sees Hanuman proudly sporting the necklace.*

**Hanuman**

Welcome, strangers.

*Rama attacks Hanuman.*

**Rama**

Where is she? Tell me? Where is she?

**Hanuman**

Help! Gods! Shiva!

**Rama**

Tell me or I'll rip your ape's head off its shoulders!

*Sugriva and Dalit enter.*

**Sugriva**
Leave him alone!

**Lakshman**
And what are you going to about it, monkey?

**Sugriva**
Monkeys can fight!

**Lakshman**
Oh yes?

**Sugriva**
Although on the other hand . . .

**Lakshman**
Coward! Stand up for your brother!

**Sugriva**
I am!

**Dalit**
Yeah, so am I.

**Lakshman**
Well, fight then!

**Sugriva**
You try fighting when you haven't eaten for four
months. Oh, just kill me now! Go on! Kill us all. In the
name of King Vali!

*He prepares to die.*

Tell my brother I died a brave simian death!

**Lakshman**
Who is King Vali?

**Rama**
What are you doing with this!
Give it to me!

**Hanuman**

No! It was a gift from the gods!

**Rama**

It was a gift to my wife from the birds of the forest!
It was around her neck when she was abducted by a
demon! Now, what is it doing around yours?

*Pause.*

**Sugriva**

So much for the chosen one.

**Dalit**

It fell from the sky on to his head.

**Rama**

Did you see who dropped it?

**Hanuman**

It fell like morning rain.

**Dalit**

He thought it was a sign from Shiva.

**Hanuman**

It is a sign! I have special powers!

**Rama**

Who are you all?

**Sugriva**

My name is Sugriva. King of the Monkeys.

**Dalit**

Ex-king.

**Sugriva**

Banished. Thrown out from my own city. By my own
brother! This is all who remain of my men. Starving
and broken. Meet the dregs of existence. Even the
untouchables won't touch us.

**Lakshman**
We too are far from our city.

**Dalit**
Which city?

**Lakshman**
Ayodhya.

**Hanuman**
Ayodhya! Holiest city in India!

**Sugriva**
Why leave such a heaven?

**Rama**
My father desired it.

**Sugriva**
Ah, I get it. Thieving? Womanising? Drinking?
It's all right, you're amongst friends.

**Lakshman**
Do you know who you speak to?

**Sugriva**
Obviously not.

**Rama**
My name is Rama, son of Dasaratha.
I have been exiled from my city Ayodhya,
My father is dead, my wife Sita abducted.
And now you see me here with my brother,
All that I have in the world.

*The Monkeys lie on the ground.*

**Monkeys**
Rama! Great king!

**Rama**
Monkeys, I need your help. I need an army,

To scour the whole of India. Every mountain, tree
and desert
Until you find my wife.

**Hanuman**

But you should ask the army of Ayodhya to help you.
We are base trash! Not fit to walk in your shadow.

**Rama**

You are exactly who I need. Who better to search
This wilderness than an army of monkeys?

**Hanuman**

Then I was chosen. I told you we were chosen!

**Sugriva**

Just one problem. I have no army of monkeys.
I don't rule Kishkindha any more. My brother does.

**Dalit**

King Vali.

**Sugriva**

And if I go back he will have my neck broken.

**Dalit**

And mine. And Hanuman's.

**Sugriva**

We're not popular.

**Rama**

What did you do to upset him?

**Sugriva**

Oh, not much.

**Dalit**

Stole his wife, country and crown.

**Sugriva**

My brother was a cruel tyrant. A monkey's life is hard.
The toughest rules.

I was his loyal second. He married a beautiful wife,
And ruled with an iron rod.

*Dalit becomes Vali, Hanuman the wife.*

Until one day, King Vali fought a demon and chased
it down a hole. Neither came back out. We waited.
A week.

**Hanuman**
A month.

**Sugriva**
A year. No sign. So I said to myself, no use crying over
spilt milk. I took the crown. The kingdom. And the
wife.

**Rama**
Ah.

**Sugriva**
It was great! The kingdom prospered. The wife saw
where her bread was buttered. We spent every day on
a bed of banana skins. Paradise! But then . . .

*Dalit pulls his head from out of the hole.*

**Dalit**
I'm back.

*Sugriva and wife Hanuman are discovered.*

**Sugriva**
From there it was all downhill. I fled the kingdom.
Now we live in this homeless misery. Every month he
sends mercenaries to kill me. Is this a life?

**Rama**
Go back.

**Sugriva**
What?

**Rama**

Kill him in single combat. Regain your kingdom and your army. And find Sita.

**Sugriva**

There's nothing I'd like more. But he's a psychopath, you see, I wouldn't stand a chance in single combat. Unless of course . . . but no, you are above trickery, and deceit . . . . It's the one way I can see to getting your wife back . . . but no, forget it.

**Rama**

What?

**Sugriva**

Say I engage him in battle, and just as he's about to beat me to a pulp, you, concealed, shoot him with your arrow. I have heard of your prowess. With Vali dead and the crown restored, I would put my army at your instant disposal. And we would not rest until Sita was reclaimed!

**Lakshman**

It is not dharma to kill through treachery.

**Sugriva**

Of course. Quite right. Forget I mentioned it.

*Pause.*

**Rama**

It is not dharma for Sita to be in the hands of slaves. Take me to Kishkindha. I will kill your king.

## SCENE TWO

*Kishkindha. Vali, King of the Monkeys, in his palace with his wife. Sugriva calls from outside the palace.*

**Sugriva**

King Vali! It's your brother Sugriva here! I have come to fight you in single combat. Fearless. Unafraid.

**Vali**

What does my coward brother think he's doing?
He's opening his arms to death. Give me my sword.

**Monkey Wife**

Don't go. There must be some trickery involved.
Send out the army and decimate them all.

**Sugriva**

Come on, brother! I'm waiting outside the city walls!
Or are you too afraid?

*He acts the chicken.*

**Vali**

Right, that's it. Give me my sword. Take my crown.

**Monkey Wife**

Stop. Think again.

**Vali**

He took the throne. He touched you.
He dies.

*She takes the crown and the two Monkeys meet for battle. Rama watches from behind a tree.*

**Sugriva**

Ah, there you are! Can't wait. The time has come . . .

**Vali**

Cut the speeches. Prepare to die.

*They fight. Viciously. Vali is stronger than Sugriva, and is about to kill him. Sugriva runs into the trees.*

**Vali**
Coward, come back! Come back and fight!

**Sugriva** (*in the trees*)
Just coming. (*To Rama.*) Why don't you shoot him?

**Rama**
I can't tell you one from another. You didn't tell me you were twins!

**Sugriva**
He's the insanely violent one!

**Rama**
It's not so easy in the blur of battle.
Wear this. I will know the difference.

*Sugriva re-enters the battlefield with a flower in his hair.*

**Vali**
You mock me?

**Sugriva**
                    I brought your wife one of these.
Just before we lay on the bed of cocoa leaves
And I entered her bright red flower . . .

*Vali roars and attacks Sugriva. A vicious battle. Rama shoots Vali in the chest.*

**Vali**
Rama? This is your doing? Why this treachery?

**Rama**
Done for the one I love and I have lost.

**Vali**
Then you will lose that love when you have found her.

*Vali dies.*

**Rama**

What did he mean? Lose her when I have found her?

**Sugriva**

Who cares? Who's going to crown me?

**Dalit**

King Vali is dead. All hail King Sugriva!

**Sugriva**

Thanks, faithful Dalit. And thanks, my noble monkeys.
I have regained my crown. And with it my wife.
Where is she? Bring honeycombs and coconuts to my
bed. It's time to party!

**Rama**

Wait, ape. Haven't you forgotten something?

**Sugriva**

I don't think so.

**Rama**

My wife! You promised to get her back.

**Lakshman**

Your side of the bargain.

**Sugriva**

Oh yes, of course. How could I have forgotten?
My army!

*A drop of rain falls.*

What's this? The rainy season starts its fall.
Now all the paths and ditches swell with flood
And all our ways become impassable.
Oh, what a shame.
Prince, noble Rama, we must wait a while.
An army cannot move through mud. Rest now,
And when the rain stops, then I'll send an army

Four thousand times five thousand flying apes
To every corner of the drying earth!
And we will find your Sita.

**Lakshman**

Rama, he's right.
An army cannot move in rainy season.

**Sugriva**

And while we wait, join us in celebration!
Eat, drink and love! Honour the death of Vali
As monkeys do, with fruit and milk and honey!

**Rama**

This was not what we agreed! Sugriva! Lakshman!

**Lakshman**

Brother, we have no choice.

**Rama**

But Sita. Sita.

*They leave. Rama stands alone as the rain falls.*


## SCENE THREE

*In Lanka, Sita is dragged into the garden of delights by Ravana.*

**Ravana**

Welcome to Lanka and this heavenly grove.
Stay here a while. Every delight is yours.
Nothing will be forced upon you. Here you are free.
And every man and woman in my court
Is at your call. Tell me what you desire.

**Sita**

To die.

**Ravana**

You are tired from the journey. I will leave you.

*Enter the servants with dresses and oils.*

My servants come to wash your aching feet.
Fine dresses, shoes and perfumes they present
To deck you like a queen.

**Sita**

I do not want them. Tell them to go away.

**Ravana**

Time is so long, sweet Sita. Such is my love
That I can wait until the earth decays
And buds again and still I'll wait, sweet Sita.
You will be mine. And freely you will choose me.

*The rain starts to fall in Lanka.*

The rainy season comes. Shelter your skin.

**Sita**

Your palace I will never enter in.

**Ravana**

Do as you wish. I am your truest friend.

*He leaves. The rain starts to fall. Sita stands under the rain.*

# Act Four

## SCENE ONE

*Kishkindha. The rain stops falling. Lakshman, Hanuman.*

**Lakshman**
It's stopped. It's stopped! It's stopped!
It's stopped! What are we waiting for? Hanuman!

**Hanuman**
My lord!

**Lakshman**
Where is my brother?

**Hanuman**
By the river. Silently weeping still.

**Lakshman**
Where's your monkey king?

**Hanuman**
Um. In bed.

**Lakshman**
In bed? But the rain has stopped!

**Hanuman**
He's drunk my lord. Too much honey! Pollutes the mind!
And there are several women with him . . . he's made
them all his queens . . . royalty's gone to his head.

**Lakshman**
Fetch him here now! Tell him my brother expects him!

**Hanuman**
Yes, my lord!

*Hanuman runs to Sugriva.*

**Hanuman**
Sugriva!

**Sugriva**
Your highness, if you please. Fig?

**Hanuman**
The rain has stopped.

**Sugriva**
A weather report from the holy monkey. Now if you don't mind . . . I'm busy.

**Hanuman**
We have to fulfil our promise!

**Sugriva**
What promise, serf?

**Hanuman**
To Prince Rama!

**Sugriva**
Oh, that.

**Hanuman**
He is in terrible pain. Every second without his wife is a needle in his heart. You've been doing nothing but drinking for three months . . .

**Sugriva**
I have been ruling my kingdom! Diktats! Decrees!

*He burps.*

**Hanuman**
You made a promise! As a monkey and as a king.

**Sugriva**
I thought he'd get over it. It's only a woman. I can supply him with plenty of alternatives.

*Enter Lakshman.*

**Lakshman**

Get out of that bed, you drunken ape!

**Sugriva**

Get him out of here. He's frightening my wives.

**Lakshman**

Remember what happened to your brother. It can happen again. Now get up!

**Sugriva**

I'll have you executed!

**Lakshman**

Just you try it! He won your kingdom for you. He can just as easily take it away again!

**Sugriva**

Oh yes, typical of the upper class. Let me tell you a story.

**Lakshman**

We don't have time for stories!

**Sugriva**

A rich man helped a poor man regain his home from bandits. The poor man and his wife settled down to sleep. Early the next morning there was a knock on the poor man's door. It was the rich man. 'I want your table as a token of your thanks.' 'But it's mine,' said the poor man. 'But I won it for you.' So the poor man gave the rich man his table. The next day the rich man came again. 'I want your roof.' 'But it's mine.' 'But I won it for you.' So the poor man gave it to him. That night he and his wife held each other tight in the wind. The third day there was a knock at the door. It was the rich man. 'I want your walls.' The poor man gave the rich man his walls without protest. Then the poor man saw the rich man looking at his wife. 'Take her now,' said the poor man. 'That way at least I won't be woken by you tomorrow morning.'

We are the pits. We have nothing. There's nothing you can take away from us.

*Enter Rama.*

**Sugriva**
Who is that man?

**Lakshman**
Do you not recognise your own deliverer?

**Sugriva**
Rama? He's as thin as a twig. What happened to him?

**Lakshman**
Grief.

**Hanuman**
Lord Rama? The rain has stopped.

**Rama**
No, I can still hear it falling.

**Hanuman**
Not so, my lord, look up. Blue sky.

**Rama**
I see only water.

**Hanuman**
In your own eyes, my lord. Take this.

*He hands him a cloth. Rama wipes his eyes.*

**Rama**
Lakshman. Tell me if it rains or not. I can still hear it.

**Lakshman**
You hear your own tears falling on the earth.

*Pause.*

**Rama**

Has it stopped?

**Sugriva**

It has, my lord. Which means one and only one thing!
Hanuman! Get these idle women out of here, this is a
time for men! Gather my army, summon monkeys
from every corner of the world! Tell them their king
commands them to quit the love-making, the banana-
munching and the honey-sucking and hot foot it here
to my court!

**Hanuman**

I go. Faster than the wind!

*Exit Hanuman.*

**Sugriva**

Sir. I thought of deceiving you.
All the sadness of the world is in your brow. It bears
no deception. We will find your Sita.

*Re-enter Hanuman.*

**Hanuman**

They come! Thousand upon thousand! A cloud of tails
dashing through the northern sky. A mountainside of
monkeys makes its way to Kishkindha!

**Sugriva**

And here they are! Welcome, friends! Welcome,
faithful apes! What a task your king has for you!
There is a princess, a paragon of beauty, this man's
wife! He fades away, of missing her. Search the earth!
Find Sita! Find the demon who took her!

Some to the West! Search in the groves and streams,
the cities and the hills. Search the hundred-peaked
mountain where winged lions sleep on the slopes.
Search the golden steppes with caves that trickle

jewels. Search the mansion on the peak of Mount
Meru where the gods worship! Ask great-souled
Varuna, who holds the noose, 'Where is Sita?' Climb
the Mountain of the Setting Sun and cry out, 'Where
is Sita?'

**Monkeys**
We go!

**Sugriva**
Some to the North! To the Himalayas and to China!
Search in the cloud-white home of Kailasa. Search in
his garden pools, filled with lotus and lily! Search in
the treeless caves of Krauncara. Search on the slopes
of Mount Mainaka where the horse-faced women
wander wild. Search in the lake of the sun-bright
swans. Search where the elephant wanders the ridges.
Search in the place with neither moon nor stars, where
a thousand streams brim with pearls and jewels.
Where the mountains blaze fire and the trees produce
clothes. Search beyond where the glow of the mountain
illuminates Brahma. Go to Brahma and ask him,
'Where is Sita?'

**Monkeys**
We go!

**Sugriva**
Some to the East! To the wooded banks of the
Kalamahi. Search in the region where the silkworm
breeds and where silver is mined. Ask the people who
have ears that cover their bodies and the people who
eat the flesh of men and the people who move on one
leg and the people who eat fish and the people who
live under water and the people who are known as
human tigers. And ask them, 'Where is Sita?'

**Monkeys**
We go!

**Sugriva**

And some to the South! To the sandalwood groves
where the river makes its way to the sea like a young
girl rushing to her lover! Search the sea-peak Puskipata
where the sun shines on one side and the moon shines
on the other. Honour it, bow before it and ask it,
'Where is Sita?' Search the path beyond the ocean that
leads to life in heaven, the realm of ancestors, the
world of Yama, hid in darkness. Go to the god of
death himself and ask him, 'Where is Sita?'

**Hanuman**

We go!

**Rama**

Hanuman! Wait.
If you find Sita, show this ring to her,
And tell her how her Rama misses her.

**Hanuman**

I will find her. Or I will die trying.

*He exits.*

**Sugriva**

Now we must wait. And until we receive news
I will not eat, nor drink, nor lie with woman.
No monkey shall. As Rama's heart starves, so shall our
    bodies.

*He leaves.*

**Lakshman**

Why still so pale? The monkeys will find her.

**Rama**

That is not the only reason for my sickness.
What if we find her? How will we find her?
Three months in a demon's court. Three months alone.
What will have become of her? Can she resist?

They have palaces and jewels of such beauty
That gods themselves have faltered. Then how can Sita
Remain untarnished?

**Lakshman**

                    Do you not trust her?

**Rama**

More than myself. More than god. And yet I doubt.

*The Monkeys of the North return.*

**Monkeys**

The Monkeys of the North return, my king!

**Sugriva**

What news?

**Monkeys**

We searched in all the places you described.
There was no sign nor word of Princess Sita.

**Rama**

No word.

**Lakshman**

It's just the North. There are three more points to the
compass.

*The Monkeys of the East return.*

**Monkeys**

The Monkeys of the East return, my king!

**Sugriva**

What news?

**Monkeys**

We searched in all the places you described.
There was no sign nor word of Princess Sita.

**Rama**

No sign.

**Monkeys**
Still the West and the South have not returned.

*The Monkeys of the West.*

The Monkeys of the West return, my lord!

**Sugriva**
What news?

**Monkeys**
We searched in all the places you described.
There was no sign nor word of Princess Sita.

*Pause.*

**Sugriva**
Hanuman and the monkeys of the South
Have not yet returned. We must wait for them.

**Rama**
This is a cruel joke the gods are playing.
Oh Hanuman. Find her. Die of hunger.
Be murdered, beaten, starved and rot. But find her!


### SCENE TWO

*The South. Hanuman and his army.*

**Hanuman**
Get up! Get up, men! We're so lost. What is this place?
Dead soil and the hiss of snakes. We have to go on!
I swore on my soul that either I bring news of Sita or
I die here in this southern dust! Always, since I was
just a little monkey, I have believed we apes were
destined for something. We have nothing, we're spat
on by man, we scavenge and scrape, we fight and
squeal and bite and scream, but always I knew we
were made for something better! But you lot! Look at

you. Wanting to die! Life is wonderful. Every painful step is a joy to me! We're all chosen by the gods. Though quite why he chose some of you is a mystery to me. Be strong. Remember Rama's face! His suffering!

*Sampatu, the vulture, brother of Jataiyu, enters and listens. One wing is lame.*

Only we can cure his pain! Others have died for it! When Sita was taken by the demon, the vulture, Jataiyu, king of the birds, flew down and tried to intervene. A mere bird! It had no chance against the demon. It gave its last breath to save Sita. And I will give mine!

**Sampatu**
Who speaks of my brother?

*Hanuman falls over.*

**Hanuman**
Haagh! Who are you?

**Sampatu**
I am Sampatu. Jataiyu's brother. Why do you speak of him?

**Hanuman**
He died in battle trying to save my lord's wife.

**Sampatu**
I know. My left wing broke of grief when I heard.

**Hanuman**
I am Hanuman, emissary of His Royal Highness King Sugriva, sent to locate the Princess Sita, wife of Rama, she whom Jataiyu tried to save!

**Sampatu**
She has not been found?

**Hanuman**
She was taken by a demon. But we don't know where!

*He falls in despair.*

**Sampatu**
But I have seen her.

**Hanuman**
You've what?

**Sampatu**
A young woman, of indescribable beauty, being carried against her will, over the ocean. By the ruler of Lanka, Ravana.

**Hanuman**
Lanka? Where is that?

**Sampatu**
Far over the ocean. Too far for me to fly.

**Hanuman**
Then how do I get there? Someone think! I have to see if she is alive! How do we get there?

Oh, you're useless!
I am the chosen one. I will go there on my own.

**Sampatu**
How will you leap an ocean, little monkey?

**Hanuman**
I am not a little monkey! I am Hanuman, chosen of Shiva! And I will make it in one leap! Watch me! From this tree I will leap to Lanka!

*Hanuman climbs the tree.*

**Monkeys**
Hanuman, stop! You'll break your neck!

**Hanuman**

I dedicate my neck to Ram and Sita! Out of my way!

**Monkeys**

No, Hanuman! No!

**Hanuman**

Jump, Hanuman! Jump!
Here I go!

*He jumps, and as he does so he becomes a giant
Monkey.*

**Monkeys**

Hanuman? What's happened to you?

**Hanuman**

Aaaaaaah! Ha ha! Didn't I tell you? I am chosen!

**Monkeys**

Hanuman! Where are you going?

**Hanuman**

Where do you think, you monkeys? To Lanka!

*And Hanuman in giant size flies over the ocean.*


SCENE THREE

*Lanka. Hanuman lands in Lanka. He returns to his
normal size.*

**Hanuman**

What is this Lanka? Everything is gold.
Perched on a mountaintop, a castle in the air.
A fortress of dreams. Ayodhya cannot match it.
It lies before me like a gorgeous woman,
The walls her firm young body, the forest her clothes,
The streams her hair and the jewelled steps and arches
Her bracelets and her earrings. I could fall in love

With Lanka. Stay in Lanka like a perfumed goddess
And breathe the sleepy succour of her skin.
No! No! Bad monkey! You are here for one reason!
Don't be sucked into this earthly heaven.
It is material. I am here for higher things.
Find Sita! And bring her to her aching love!

*He enters the palace. Many women lie, semi-clothed,
in a sleep of desire.*

Who are these goddesses?
Flushed with completed pleasure, sleeping deeply.
Their clothes in disarray. One has lost an anklet,
Another's pearls lie scattered on the floor,
Their tinkling ornaments rest on their breasts
Like birds on a silent pool after a storm.
Ravana's wives! Still hot with his desire.
Overcome with love and heat and alcohol.
Some kiss each other thinking they are him.
Some languish naked like mares rolling on grass,
Hips and thighs pressed to each other.
What if Sita is one of them? What if she has succumbed?
Impossible! But I must check. I can't see them.
Careful, monkey. If one of them wakes, you die.

*Hanuman checks the women.*

Oh, such beauty. Resist the flesh, Hanuman.
Think of the spirit. Look for moon-bright Sita.
No, she's not here. Not here. Nor here. Oh, pure Sita!
Where then? How will I find her?
If I don't, I'll drown myself in the ocean!
What's through this golden archway? I hear birdsong.

*He enters the grove. Sita stands alone in her rags.*

It's her.
I see his face in her eye. The same despair.
So thin that she might almost disappear.
Oh Hanuman, restore her with your news!

*Ravana enters.*

Someone comes. Hide, monkey, in the ashoka tree!

*Hanuman hides in the trees.*

**Ravana**
It is three months now you have not tasted food.
I worry for your health.

**Sita**
Then let me go.

**Ravana**
I cannot. I have fallen in love with you.
And every day you fast and waste away
My love grows, as if fed by you.

**Sita**
You told me am I free.

**Ravana**
Not this again.

**Sita**
Then give me freedom to leave this land
Or to kill myself.

**Ravana**
What freedom is that?
I offer you the freedom from your bonds,
The bonds of received wisdom. The world of Ayodhya
Is foolish superstition and belief
That keeps its people in hunger and deprivation
Under the banner of goodness. Belief is a trick
Cheaper than bread, and while we swallow it
The ancient powers will feed us this religion
While in their larders they pile up cakes and wine.

**Sita**
Rama keeps nothing for himself.

**Ravana**

Rama is good but he is not yet king.
Kings change the moment a crown is on their head.

**Sita**

You are king here.

**Ravana**

But I encourage business.
Expansion. The individual.
The pursuit of happiness. The satisfaction
Of achieved desire. People want for nothing.
They are happier in Lanka than in Ayodhya
Their clothes are finer. Their food is full of goodness.
Disease is cured and death a distant cousin.
In Ayodhya, death knocks at every door
And people have no means to keep it out.
There they die, here we live.
There they have nothing. Here we have everything.

**Sita**

Then why do you need me?

**Ravana**

                    I need a queen.

**Sita**

Take one of your wives. They are all so beautiful.

**Ravana**

A dime a dozen. You are the one I want.

**Sita**

You want me only because I refuse you.
The moment I give this body to you, you'll be bored.
That is the curse of freedom. When you can have
    everything
You only want the thing beyond your reach.

**Ravana**

You're denying yourself such happiness.
Soft sheets, sweet perfumes.

**Sita**

I care for none of it.

**Ravana**

And love! I love better than any man.
I will attend to your every desire.
Your body I will worship as a shrine.

**Sita**

Please do not touch me.

**Ravana**

You cannot prevent it.

**Sita**

I trust your promise to me. Freely given.

**Ravana**

I can leave you in this garden here for ever
To wither like a starved plant. And when you die
I'll not allow a soul to enter in.
No burial or honorary burning
Will I allow.
I'll let the ravens come and peck your flesh
And your bones will rot in the dust.

**Sita**

Please do not touch me.

**Ravana**

I cannot stop myself. I am in torture.

**Sita**

I am sorry.

**Ravana**

            Ever since I saw your face

Everything I have created and amassed
Means nothing to me.

**Sita**

                          You have good reason
Then to be angry with me. I am destroying you
As much as you are decimating me.

**Ravana**

Oh Sita. Hold me. Please.

**Sita**

I cannot.

**Ravana**

Offer some pity!

**Sita**

I offer pity.

**Ravana**

With your flesh!

**Sita**

I have no flesh to give. I am pure bone.

**Ravana**

Your heart, then.

**Sita**

It belongs to Rama.

**Ravana**

Take it back!

**Sita**

It is not mine to take. It belongs to Rama.

**Ravana**

Don't say that name, or I'll stop your tongue for ever!
I must apologise. I made a promise
I cannot keep. I said I would not force you

To be my lover, but that I would wait
For you to freely come. I cannot do this.
You have one month. You will be left alone.
No food. No human company. If at the end of which
You do not knock on my door, plead forgiveness,
Offer yourself to me freely, of your own will –
I'll take you by force. Then, valueless,
I'll throw you to my men to use you up
Then butcher you, cut you in little pieces
And boil you (or what little there is left)
For my morning meal. Have a think about it.
And in a month I'll be listening at my door.

*He leaves.*

**Sita**

Hard heart. Why don't you shatter into a thousand
　　pieces?
Where are you, gods? I have followed dharma.
I have stayed true to the ways taught by father,
The ways of Ayodhya. Truth! Honesty! Where are you?
Where is my Rama? Dead probably! Killed by beasts
Or Ravana's men. And all our hopes in shreds!
I will not live to see it. Not to see Lanka raze
Ayodhya to the ground. Not to see the dawning
Of the age of Kali when death shall stalk the earth
With golden skulls hung round her jewelled neck.
I'll break my own before I see such horror.

*She pulls at her own clothes and rips her rags into a
noose. She tries to hang herself from a tree. It is the
tree Hanuman is hiding in, and he falls on to her.*

**Hanuman**

What are you doing, Princess?

**Sita**

Killing myself. Away from me, monkey! Leave me to die!

**Hanuman**

But Princess Sita!

**Sita**

Scram! Leave me alone!
You know my name. Who are you? What do you want?

**Hanuman**

My name is Hanuman, oh great Princess.

**Sita**

Get up from the ground. There is no royalty here.

**Hanuman**

There is the wife of Rama.

**Sita**

You know Rama?

**Hanuman**

He is my lord.

**Sita**

Ah no. This is a trick of Ravana's.
He has taken another form.

**Hanuman**

Mistress. It is not so.

**Sita**

Monkey, if you lie, I'll take your tail
And wind it around your miserable neck
And hang you till you choke!

*Hanuman holds out the ring.*

**Sita**

What is that?

**Hanuman**

Do you not recognise it?

**Sita**

It cannot be. His ring. It cannot be.

**Hanuman**
It is.

**Sita**
Give it me.
And if I could I'd force it into my breast
So it could rest in my heart. Oh Rama. Rama.
How is he? Does he live? Is he sick? Or well?
Has he died of grief? Of longing? Why don't you speak?

**Hanuman**
I was just waiting for a space to do so.
Mistress, he waits for you. An army of monkeys
He sent to find you! I am one such ape,
The lowest, poorest creature, but he chose me.

**Sita**
You are not poor! You are magnificent!
You are a monkey god! How did you get here?

**Hanuman**
I jumped.

**Sita**
                    The ocean?

**Hanuman**
                              In one bound. It was nothing.

**Sita**
And this is a lowest creature?

**Hanuman**
                              Why are you crying?
Tears stream from your eyes like water from a broken
    pot.

**Sita**
Does he still love me?

**Hanuman**
Does the sun shine? Do monkeys get drunk on honey?

When the rains fell he would not come inside,
But stayed by the river alone, freezing to death.

**Sita**

I did the same.

**Hanuman**

And now you both have colds.
Jump on my back! I'll take you back to him!

*Pause.*

Mistress, let's not delay. Soldiers may come.
Or worse, the king himself. Any monkey can see
The man dies of impatience. We need to go.

**Sita**

I am not going with you.

**Hanuman**

                    Mistress, forgive me
If I appear astounded by your words.
I thought that you were rather keen to see him.

**Sita**

Rama must fetch me. That is what dharma decrees.
A king does not send envoys to do his work.
Go back to your lord, tell him where I am.
And tell him Sita waits for him to fetch her.

**Hanuman**

Mistress, I act upon your every word
And yet it seems to me to be much easier
If you'd just hop on board. Why dot every i?

**Sita**

Foolish monkey. You have not been to Ayodhya.
You have not seen the river gently breathe
Its wisdom into every human heart.
If you had, you would know that it must be
That Rama alone shall come and rescue Sita.

**Hanuman**

But mistress . . . it's just . . . I'm here. I can leap oceans.

**Sita**

Enough! No more words. Tell him he has a month
To come and fetch his long-awaited Sita
Before Ravana feasts upon her flesh.

**Hanuman**

Why take such risks?

**Sita**

Nothing is won without risk.
Take my ring back and burn it in his heart.
And take this kiss and give it him. Now go!

SCENE FOUR

*Kishkindha. Rama alone by the river.*

**Rama**

The monkeys have not come. Sita is dead.
Or worse, she has fallen into a demon's arms.
Why is this doubt pursuing me? Better she is dead
Than that I find her awoken to some other's charms.
A richer city. Happier, more beautiful.
Ayodhya is dying.
The world no longer needs its ancient wisdom.
Lakshman lies sleeping. I have taken this chance.
To come down to the river and drown myself.
I am as weary of the world as it is of Ayodhya.

*He is about to leap when he hears . . . .*

**Lakshman**

Rama!

**Rama**

Do it now, Rama. Do not be deterred.

**Lakshman**
Hanuman has returned!

**Rama**
What did he say?

*Enter Lakshman.*

**Lakshman**
What are you doing? Hanuman is back!

*Enter all the Monkeys in a babble.*

**Sugriva**
My lord. My man Hanuman has returned!
And with him, oh fantastic news! Tell him. Tell him.

**Rama**
Hanuman?

**Sugriva**
Come on man, spit it out!

**Hanuman**
I have found her.

**Sugriva**
You see? Didn't I say he would? The monkey found her!

**Lakshman**
Brother. Did you not hear him?

**Rama**
Lakshman,
Did you ask him to say this? To save my life?

**Lakshman**
No, brother.

**Rama**
This is not a generous trick.
To keep me on this godforsaken earth.

**Monkeys**

No, Rama. It's not a trick. Look.

*Hanuman presents the ring. Rama crumples.*

**Rama**

Oh dear gods, forgive my dreadful thought.
Oh Hanuman, where is she?

**Hanuman**

She's in Lanka.

**Rama**

Ravana's island.

**Hanuman**

It was he who took her.
He wants her for his queen, but she refused.
In a lonely grove she lingers, pale as snow.
She has not taken food for ninety days.

**Lakshman**

You spoke to her? Then why didn't you bring her?

**Sugriva**

You stupid gibbon. Leaving her like that.
I ought to have you shot!

**Hanuman**

I tried to bring her,
But she refused. She insists that Rama comes
And brings her back himself.

**Rama**

She is right.
If you had brought her back here on your own
I would have killed you with my naked hands.

**Hanuman**

See? She was exactly the same.

**Rama**
    I am a king. I represent Ayodhya.
    And in Ayodhya's name I will conquer Lanka,
    Murder that grasping demagogue who rules it
    And bring back my queen. Take me to the ocean.

# Act Five

*Ram on the cliff.*

**Rama**

Ocean, why don't you part? I have been here
A month! Waiting for you! Stoical and calm.
These virtues mean nothing to you, friend of Lanka!
Patience is weakness in this world. Now time
Is running out. Sita's about to die!
Answer me or I'll declare war on you.
I'll flood your waters with a thousand arrows,
Make carcasses of fish overflow your shores,
Then burn your waters with a searing heat
Till they dry up into a scorched desert
And every creature that exists inside
Chokes on the dust of your ingratitude
That will not part for Rama and his army!

*Ram prepares his weapon. The Ocean speaks.*

**Ocean**

Rama, be calm. I cannot part for you.
I have my nature. To let you walk right through
Would be to deny myself. Would you wish that?

**Rama**

But without Sita I cannot be myself.

**Ocean**

Then build a bridge of stepping stones across me.
I will not let them sink. The sea monsters
That patrol my depths shall not attack you.
Call your army.

85

**Rama**

Monkeys! Get rocks! Trees! Anything you can find!
Build a bridge of stepping stones from here to Lanka.

**Hanuman**

What is five thousand miles of wild water
When Rama yearns for Sita! Build the bridge!

*The bridge is built and Rama crosses the ocean.*


SCENE TWO

*Lanka. The garden. Sita alone. Wasted and weak.
Ravana enters.*

**Ravana**

A month has passed. You did not knock at my door.

**Sita**

And never will.

**Ravana**

You remember what I said?

**Sita**

I remember.

**Ravana**

You are so weak from hunger.
I can take you by force. I can do what I want with you.

**Sita**

Then we both lose. I my life. You your soul.

**Ravana**

I care not.

**Sita**

Then take me. I will not resist.
But you will not have my mind.

*Ravana touches her.*

**Ravana**
You are mine now.

**Sita**
                    Oh Rama. Sweet Rama.

**Ravana**
Silence. Don't mention his name.

**Sita**
Oh Rama. Sweet Rama. I can feel you.

**Ravana**
I said be quiet. Or I'll strangle you.

**Sita**
Then do it! Coward! Do it now! Kill me!
Then I'll be silent. Then you can have your way
Without my interruption. Slit my throat.
Or it will utter Rama Rama Rama
Until I die and Rama Rama Rama

**Ravana**
Shut up! Shut up!

**Sita**
                    No, I am not afraid.
Your freedom is nothing but a fear of death.
A desperate desire to prolong life
In the face of dying's dark necessity.
But I have faith. Death is not death to me.
Then what have I to fear? You cannot win.
Oh Rama. Rama. Rama.

**Ravana**
                    I'll shut your mouth.

*He moves to kill her. Rama calls out from the bridge.*

87

**Rama**

Ravana, I have to come to get back my wife.

**Ravana**

Take the Princess and lock her in my chambers.

*They take her away.*

Rama, you have saved me from atrocity.
Now I will do what I do best. Destroy you.
Call up my army! Prepare to annihilate
This mystic and his army of Ayodhya.

**Rama**

I do not bring an ordinary army.
Prepare to fight as you have never fought.

*Rama and his army of Monkeys invade Ayodhya.*
*A furious battle. Ravana is losing. He is met by*
*an Officer.*

**Officer**

General, these monkeys are too quick for our swords.
We have never fought like this! They fly through the air,
Now on the roofs, now in the streets. Our traditional
    ways
That have conquered kingdoms are too slow and heavy.
We are losing men in this guerrilla warfare.

**Ravana**

Then we must find some other way to beat them.
Call up my brother Indrajit the trickster.

**Indrajit**

You need but ask, my lord, and I am here.

**Ravana**

Indrajit, use your art to carve a statue,
A living, breathing Sita. Make it of clay.
Make it so fine that he will think it Sita.
Bring it before me.

**Indrajit**

Brother it is done.

*The Maya Sita appears.*

**Ravana**

Bring her into battle so all may see her there!

*The Maya Sita is brought into battle.*

**Rama**

Tyrant, why do you bring my wife into the field?

**Ravana**

Is she your wife? Then I apologise.
For what I now must do.

*He cuts off the Maya Sita's head. Rama stops dead.*

Fight on, my lord. Or have you lost the will?

**Lakshman**

Rama! Don't drop your guard!

*Ravana shoots Rama with his arrow. Lakshman runs
in front and falls.*

**Rama**

He's dead. Oh brother. Oh my loyal brother.
Hanuman. Sound the retreat. Say all is lost.

**Hanuman**

Must I do this?

**Rama**

What else? My city's lost.
My father dead. My Sita. Now my Lakshman.
My very self. My heart . . .

*He falls.*

**Hanuman**

His heart has broken.

**Ravana**

Take me to Sita. I want to show her her love.

*Exit.*

**Hanuman**

I will go sound the retreat.

**Sugriva**

Do no such thing! Hanuman, god of monkeys. You can save us.

**Hanuman**

What can I do?

**Sugriva**

Grow to your giant size and fly over the ocean. Head for the Herb Mountain. It contains every medicine. There are four we need. The mrtyasanjivani. The visalyakarni. The sauvarnakarni and the samdhani. Collect all four and bring them back!

**Hanuman**

I grow, I go. Oh Rama. Hold that heart!

*He exits. Ravana enters, dragging Sita, unseen by the others.*

**Sita**

Where is he?

**Ravana**

There is your love. I told you you could see him.

**Sita**

Dead?

**Ravana**

It would appear so.

**Sita**

Let me go to him!

**Ravana**
No. Freedom has its limits. Take her inside.
I'll finish off this battle. Then come to you
And claim you as my spoils.

**Sita**
                                    Just let me die.
Please let me die.

**Ravana**
                        Eventually. Take her.


SCENE THREE

*The Mountain of Herbs. Hanuman stands by the mountain.*

**Hanuman**
This is the Herb Mountain. I've remembered the names
of the herbs. The mrtyasanjivani. The visalyakarni.
The sauvarnakarni and the samdhani. Let's start
looking.

*He looks at the mountain.*

There are thousands of them! All virtually identical!
Which ones are they? What if I take the wrong one?
Then dear, sweet Ram, my lord, incarnation of gods,
Will die! And it will be my fault! My fault!

Bugger it, I'll take the whole mountain.

Fly, Hanuman. Fly!

## SCENE FOUR

*Lanka. Ram and Lakshman lie dead. The Monkeys.*
*Ravana enters.*

**Ravana**
Why this pause in battle? Let's re-engage.

**Sugriva**
You killed my noble lord through trickery.

**Ravana**
You apes don't exactly fight by the book.
Fight, or surrender everything to me.
The crown, the queen, the whole of Ayodhya.

**Sugriva**
We'll fight until the last monkey drops.

**Ravana**
You do that. Then I'll take your skins and make
A coat for every citizen of Lanka.
Prepare the attack!

*Ravana exits. Hanuman flies in.*

**Hanuman**
Aaaaahhhh!
Sorry, I didn't want to waste a second.

**Sugriva**
Where are the herbs?

**Hanuman**
I didn't know which ones to pick! There were thousands!
And so I brought the mountain.

*A cascade of herbs falls on the stage. Sugriva searches.*

**Sugriva**
These are them.

*He squeezes them in Rama's and Lakshman's eyes.*
*They wake.*

**Rama**
Sita? Is she dead?

**Lakshman**
Brother, you live.

**Rama**
I live if you do. Why has the battle stopped?
Do we have Sita? Is she dead or alive?

**Lakshman**
You know we saw her die.

**Rama**
Where is her body?

**Hanuman**
We do not know.

**Rama**
Then attack! Fight, bite, rip limbs
And murder flesh until we have found Sita.

*Ravana enters. He sees Rama.*

**Ravana**
I see a ghost.

**Rama**
Lanka doesn't believe in ghosts.
That's ancient wisdom, stuff for fools. Remember?
And since there are no gods, no gods can help me.
It will be me alone who will reclaim my wife
Alive or dead.

*The final battle. Ravana and his men are killed. Rama
kills Ravana. The Monkeys tear the flesh of Ravana.*

**Sugriva**
The demon is dead and all his men! Ha ha!

**Hanuman**
I have lit my tail with fire and leapt from golden roof
to golden roof, garden to garden, street to street. The
whole of Lanka burns! Ours is the victory!

**Lakshman**
Take Ravana away and give him last rites.

**Sugriva**
Last rites for this thug? Let's just spit on him and
chuck him in a ditch.

**Rama**
He was a brave man. He looked for freedom.
His cruelty was only so extreme
Because he could not find it. Give him last rites.

*The Monkeys take Ravana away.*

Hanuman. Wait. Search the palace.
Look for my wife's body. Bring it here.

*Hanuman exits.*

Lakshman, return to Ayodhya with your men.
I will stay here and mourn my wife a while.

**Lakshman**
How long, brother?

**Rama**
                    A little while maybe.
A month or so, maybe a year, or three,
Or ten, or three score five, or all my life . . .

*Hanuman brings Sita.*

**Sita**
I saw him dead. Do not deceive me, monkey.

**Hanuman**
Look up, sweet mistress. I do not deceive you.

*Sita looks up.*

Did I not say? Today's a day of miracles.

**Lakshman**
Brother, look up.

**Rama**
Let me keep my eyes on Sita in the earth.

**Lakshman**
Look up in the air and feast your eyes on Sita.

*Rama looks up.*

**Rama**
Is this a dream? My Sita is dead.

**Sita**
My Ram is dead.

**Rama**
Ravana cut her head off. Did we not see it?

**Hanuman**
It was a trick, my lord. An effigy.

**Sita**
And you were dead right there upon the ground.

**Rama**
This wondrous monkey brought me herbs to cure me.

**Sita**
Then we both live again.

*Sugriva and the Monkeys enter.*

**Sugriva**
Last rites completed. Rather against my will.
What have we here? Oh, she's alive! Oh yes!
How the hell did she do that!

**Sita**

Ravana is dead?

**Rama**

Yes, he is dead.

**Sita**

I mourn him.

**Sugriva**

No time for mourning. Let's go celebrate!

**Lakshman**

Go to her, brother.

*Pause.*

**Hanuman**

Go to your queen, my lord.

**Sita**

If it is too much for you to bear, I will come to you.

*She approaches Rama. He turns away.*

**Hanuman**

What is it, my lord? You have found your love.

**Lakshman**

This is a time for joy!

**Rama**

You mourn Ravana?

**Sita**

What is it, my lord?

**Rama**

You said yourself. You mourn him. Why do you
mourn him?

**Sita**

I grieve for a troubled soul.

**Rama**

You mourn a friend!

*Pause.*

I have killed my enemy and avenged my insult.
But it was not for your sake. It was for my honour.
And for my family. I have doubts about you.
You have been here for many months.
You have tasted the joys of Lanka and its wealth.
You have enjoyed Ravana's company
Enough to weep over his dying body.

**Sita**

Not so. Lakshman, monkeys, tell him it is not so.

**Rama**

Leave me. You are free to go wherever you want.
How can a man of pure descent live with a woman
Who has been another king's willing concubine?

**Lakshman**

Brother, what is this madness that you speak?

**Hanuman**

Sugriva, this is your brother's curse that haunts him.
'Then you will lose your love when you have found it!'

**Rama**

Did he touch you?

**Sita**

If he did it was against my will.

**Rama**

Ravana took you for a reason. You don't catch fish
Purely to look at them. Did he touch you?

**Sita**

How can you say such things to me? You should know
better.
I starved for you. I resisted all advances.

**Rama**

Did he touch you?

**Sita**

He never touched my heart!
Those other parts of me I did not own.
I was in captivity. A woman kept
Against her will no longer owns her body,
Only her mind and soul.

**Rama**

He did touch you.
And all Ayodhya will know it. And will whisper it.
Ravana's concubine. Now Rama's wife.
You have been in Lanka too long. You are tainted.
Leave now. Go! Out of my sight. Southern whore.

**Sita**

Lakshman. Clear a circle. Build a pyre.

**Lakshman**

But Sita . . .

**Sita**

Do it. Light the fire.

*Lakshman builds a pyre and lights it.*

If my heart has strayed, then let this fire consume me.

*She walks into the fire.*

**Lakshman**

Sita! My lord tell me to put out the fire.

**Hanuman**

Mistress, no! No! Rama! Wake up from this spell!

**Sugriva**

Put out the fire, my lord!

**Hanuman**
Wake up! Wake from this madness! It is the curse of Vali that torments you. Break that jealous curse with all your strength, great lord. Reason must balance with belief!

*Rama looks into the fire.*

**Rama**
Do not put out the fire.

**Lakshman**
My lord, tell me to put out the fire.

**Hanuman**
Put out the fire!

**Rama**
Do not put out the fire!

*He enters the fire.*

**Lakshman**
Brother, no!

*The fire consumes Rama and Sita. The Monkeys wail. A rain falls.*

**Sugriva**
Rain? It is not the rainy season.

**Hanuman**
Rain from the gods!

**Lakshman**
The fire dies down!

**Hanuman**
Look! Sita is unharmed!

**Lakshman**
And Rama too!

**Hanuman**

They have become gods! Perfection made more perfect!
Oh mistress! Oh my lord!

**Rama**

Lead us back to Ayodhya. Rama and his queen.
Light lamps and candles, diyas and holy lanterns,
That every flame may welcome Sita home,
And may the ancient river shimmer still
That all shall be forgiven.

*The End.*